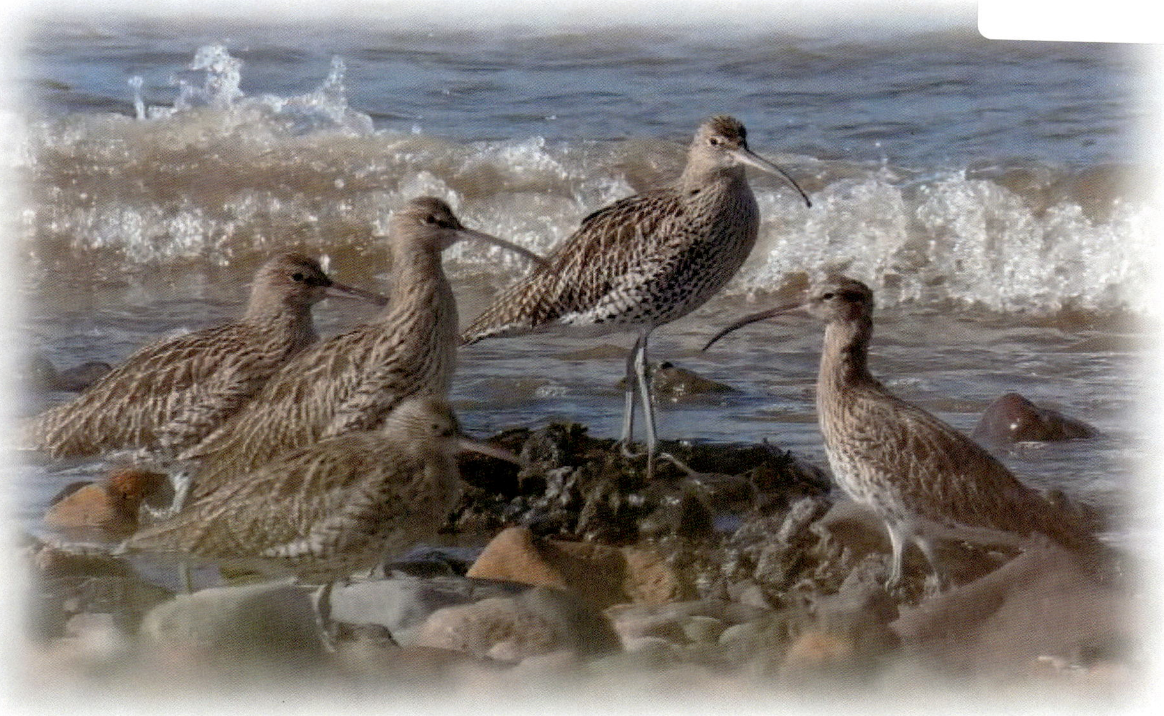

Some of My Birds
Avian Therapy in West Cumbria

David Murray

Family & Friends Limited Edition
December 2022

Copyright © 2022 David John Murray

Published by: David John Murray
books@davidmurray.org.uk

All rights reserved.
No part of this publication may be reproduced,
stored in a retrieval system, or transmitted
in any form or by any means, electronic,
mechanical, photocopying, recording or otherwise,
without the prior permission of the publisher.

First published 2022

ISBN: 9798367770865
Independently published
by David John Murray, Workington

Contents

Foreword

1. Where I Walk

2. Birds I See Most

3. Birds at the Shoreline: Waders

4. Birds in the Bushes: Perching Birds, Passerines

5. A Little Larology - A Galaxy of Gulls

6. Birds on the Pond: Ducks, Geese, Swans and More

7. Birds by the River and Stream

8. A Closing Miscellany

A Few Pages For Notes

Foreword

This book is intended to encourage people to explore the area in which they live and to see things that previously they would have walked past, blissfully unaware of their existence. Until recent years that was me so far as most wildlife was concerned .

Secondly, it aims to show just one aspect of this wonderful area of Cumbria. Most people in Britain know of the Lake District, even if on TV quiz programmes they can't always locate it on the map, but Cumbria is much more than the Lake District. Since retiring back to the North after some years in the East Midlands I've had the privilege of living in two areas of the county which are *not* "the Lakes" - the beautiful Eden Valley and now the West Cumbria coast. These wonderful areas are inadequately known and explored.

From the outset I must make it very clear that *I am neither an expert ornithologist nor a professional photographer*. As to photography I had previously dabbled in landscapes but until 2020 had never attempted photographing wildlife of any kind. As to birds it would not be too much of a wild exaggeration to say that I scarcely knew an oystercatcher from an ostrich.

So how on earth do I come to be authoring this book? **It's all the fault of the Coronavirus!** Being in the second half of my seventies and suffering from asthma I stayed very strictly at home for many weeks, hiding from the virus even when we were encouraged to go out for exercise walks. Weekly appearances in the church pulpit were replaced by service and sermon videos made in my home study, which was transformed into a recording studio. ... And I grew heavier and heavier!

Something had to be done, but brisk circular walks around the streets of Workington wearing a mask quickly lost their appeal. Having at that stage lived in the area for less than a year I didn't know much about the town's surroundings, but a study of the local Ordnance Survey map, led to my asking myself, "Why not explore some of the areas just outside the town? And why not take a camera?"

Well the rest, as they say, is history and before long I was sharing photographs of birds with friends on my Facebook page.

Why this book? It's one thing to take some pictures for one's own entertainment, but another to put them into a book. The first person to suggest to me that my Facebook bird photographs should be published as a book was an old friend and former senior colleague in the anti-corruption movement. I'm sorry Peter, I've no idea when or whether that project history you suggested will ever see the light of day, but here at least are the birds.

As well as Peter, another very good friend Margaret has been a great supporter of my bird photography from the beginning. In particular she encouraged me when I started including narrative remarks along with the pictures. This book is something of an expansion of that model.

So what equipment do I use? The photos were mostly taken using new, modern cameras and lenses, bought after getting much more than expected compensation money from a bank. However, mixed with them are some taken with my old equipment, bought well over a decade ago. I challenge you to spot the difference. It is not necessary to have the latest semi-professional kit to get enjoyable photos, although better equipment does make possible some shots that otherwise would be unachievable.

The camera with which I started is a Nikon D3000 single-lens reflex (SLR for short) along with a Tamron telephoto lens that zooms from 70 mm to 300 mm.

The core of my newer *walk-about kit* is a Nikon D7500 camera body. It's still within the "hobbyist" bracket rather than professional, although some professionals speak highly of it. Amongst improvements are faster focusing and better handling of the low light conditions which are not uncommon here in the north-west The lens is another Tamron, zooming from 18 mm wide angle to 400 mm telephoto. It is certainly heavier than the old equipment, but I find it easy enough to carry attached to a wrist strap. It doesn't need a shoulder harness although sometimes to allow for more hands-free activity I do use one.

Then there's the "big boy", the Sigma 150-600 mm *long-telephoto* zoom lens. This is for working at a far distance or to fill the frame with a single bird at shorter distance. It's a brilliant lens, but it's heavy! I usually carry it on a **shoulder strap** (*never* a neck strap!) but if I'm going to be out with it for several hours I sometimes use a chest harness that carries the weight more comfortably over long periods. To avoid constantly changing the D7500 back and forth between the two lenses I eventually bought a cheap second-hand Nikon D600 to stay permanently on the long lens and this gives me good results.

One other point. People ask me whether I use a **tripod**, especially with the heavier lens. The answer is, "Sometimes", but I find carrying the tripod around for hours to be too inconvenient although for a while I experimented with carrying everything in a converted shopping trolley. I do have a **backpack** with tripod strap but don't often use it, so almost all of the images in the book were shot hand-held. Yes, it takes practice to hold a long lens still enough but you get there eventually.

I said above, "enjoyable photographs". The pictures here in the book are not processed to become works of art. They are designed simply to reflect what was seen on the day. They are meant to be "real", not idealised images of a world that doesn't exist.

This collection is a kind of summary of what I now know of a world that I'd been walking past blindly for over seventy years. The exercise and the mental relaxation have been truly therapeutic. Time with the birds has cleared my mind and slimmed my body. You might prefer another subject, maybe flora rather than fauna, or landscapes or townscapes, or whatever takes your fancy. Whatever the theme, getting out on foot with camera (or sketch pad?) brings physical and mental benefit. I recommend it.

David Murray, Workington, December 2022

1.

Where I Walk

At the outset I should define my geographical area. Firstly there are the places where I have walked often, that are accessible from home in Workington within a matter of minutes in the car. (No I have not, in my late-70s, returned to cycling.) This patch extends from around Whitehaven to just north of Maryport. Secondly, areas further north as far as Bowness-on-Solway and Port Carlisle (not to be confused with the city of Carlisle!).

Living by the coast I walk by **the seashore**, and in West Cumbria we're blessed with a lot of it in considerable variety, pebbly beaches, sandy shores, dunes, cliffs and headlands. Some of this is natural, though agriculturally influenced, whereas other parts have been significantly shaped by the region's old and now defunct industries, coal, iron and steel, which also led to the construction of **harbours**, like this one at Harrington, with glorious mud from which waders feed.

A few hundred yards inland we have **ponds.** The Siddick Ponds nature reserve behind Workington's ASDA store is a great example of old industrial reservoirs repurposed for nature. Also at Workington we not only have the Derwent estuary but inland there are great walks by the **river** as it brings the water from the Borrowdale Valley, Derwentwater, Bassenthwaite Lake, Crummock Water and more through Workington into the Solway Firth and the Irish Sea.

Wherever you go there are **bushes and trees**. There's a small nature reserve at Crosscanonby north of Maryport with woodland. By **paths** along old railway track, now cycle paths, there are birds. And here is a view in the Harrington reserve.

Top: View looking south east over Siddick Pond with Lake District mountains in the far distance.
Bottom: The lower, smaller pond at Siddick showing the old railway bridge between the ponds.
(Both photos in March/April)

A bright but cloudy April day at the north end of Maryport promenade, looking across the Solway to Scotland. I've taken many a bird photo on these sands and rocks - Gulls, Oystercatchers, Redshanks, Curlews, Herons, and more.

Down at the Shoreline

Some of my first explorations were to the Northside, or Oldside, shore at Workington. It was a delight to be able to drive to the old car park then walk along the shore to the far headland to watch birds feed at the edge of the tide.

Another early shore visit was to the Skinburness end of the Silloth promenade and it was here that I first saw *Turnstones* (above). I had no idea what they were but loved the rich tones of their summer plumage. Very often I turned to the UK bird identification group on Facebook for advice. I still use it quite often. The members are helpful and very rarely does anyone mind being asked a stupid question.

If my ignorance of bird life was almost total my understanding of the key techniques of wildlife photography matched it. As explained in the Foreword I started off with old equipment. Only when confident that I really would continue with the new hobby did I invest in anything new and expensive.

Other birds in those early days included **Ringed Plovers** (above). Soon afterwards, near Bowness-on-Solway I saw my first ringed bird and was able to report its details to the researchers, a ringed Ringed Plover. This little bird (below) proved to be only a few months old but already to have flown across the North Sea and the North of England to the Solway Coast. I wonder where it went next.

It was not long before I started to recognise more waders from the shoreline such as Redshanks, Oystercatchers and Curlews.

Then there were others apart from Waders. The Derwent estuary by the port is popular with Cormorants, especially in the winter. Grey Herons are seen at the coast as well as inland on ponds and streams; also their cousins, Little Egrets.

To write much about gulls is more than I should attempt here. From the early months there were Herring Gulls, Black-Headed Gulls, Great Black-Backed Gulls, Lesser Black-Backed Gulls, and occasionally Mediterranean Gulls (below). Distinguishing between these species as adults did not prove difficult, but when it came to immature birds it was a different matter. A Herring Gull, for example, is not fully mature until five years old and changes plumage every year. More on these later, and I must not forget to mention the little birds such as Rock Pipits, Pied Wagtails, and more. We shall meet them as we go along.

These two *Mediterranean Gulls* were part of a small flock on the seaweed opposite the Port of Workington. Being July they have their black heads for the breeding season. In winter they have only a dark smudge behind the eye. (A winter Black-headed Gull, in contrast, has a more clearly defined black dot behind the eye and also has black wing-tips). And what have we in the bottom left of the picture?

You may have noticed that the Mediterranean Gulls image is not just as sharp as some others. I considered replacing it, but have left it here to illustrate a point. Even with better equipment it hasn't always been easy to get perfect shots. In this case the birds were so far away in poor light that even with the 600 mm lens they only showed up very small in the centre of the original picture. To show it here I've cut out that centre part, blown it up in size, and used software to sharpen the image as best I could. Sometimes that's all one can do.

Although we'll look at gulls more closely later on I think it would be remiss of me to show only the less frequently seen Mediterranean Gull and not show one of the more regular birds. So just to finish off this chapter, here's a *Great Black-backed Gull* surrounded by *Herring Gulls*. You'll see what a big powerful-looking bird this is.

The photo above was taken at Maryport, close to the point shown on page 7, but one of my areas for Great Black-backed Gulls due to its proximity to home is the shore at Workington, especially the estuary of the River Derwent opposite the port gates. This is outstandingly the best place I know of for observing them when they come to feed at the mouth of the river as the tide changes.

The view above, looking down from the hill, shows the modern port. Until recent years in the area to the right of the picture on the near side was the steel works which had its own dockside on this side of the water a little to the left, now crumbling. My bird photographs include images from every watery point in this area, except for the port itself, and especially on the sloping pebble and seaweed water's edge on this side of the channel. The centuries-old harbour is off the river on the near side to the right and stretches inland almost to the railway station.

Walking by the Pond

On arrival at Siddick Pond, after walking from the car park, the first birds seen are very often swans. However, peering through a gap in the shrubbery the pond depth gauge comes into view and quite often it's occupied More than nine times out of ten the bird in occupation is a Cormorant. Occasionally another bird may have taken the spot. I've seen it twice. It really is Cormorant territory.

Often the next birds to be seen are Greylag Geese (left). These breed each year, so that in spring and early summer sizeable families of goslings are to be seen on both the larger and smaller areas of the pond. The group shown opposite, though, seemed to arrive as a flight from the north just a few minutes earlier.

I'll leave the variety of Ducks, Grebes. Coots and Moorhens until later, but must mention swans. Usually that means Mute Swans. They are the swans most commonly found in England, but there are others to be seen (chapter 6). During the summer months there are cygnets, and many survive to become adults. This shot of a Mute Swan in flight was taken in January.

Strolling along the River

The most common riverside spot for me is the River Derwent by the Mill Field upstream of Workington Bridge and as far as the Yearl weir. On the other side of the river it is possible to walk further and that is something I do from time to time.

Simply because they are so common there can be a tendency to ignore the Mallards, but we mustn't do that. They're interesting birds and, in my opinion at least, attractive in appearance. Here is a male and two females on the relatively still water above the weir on a cold winter morning.

Below the weir there is an island. The river flows down two sides of it and where the two streams join there is a pebble bank. Often Goosanders are to be seen resting or walking around on the pebbles while at the water's margin a Common Sandpiper (below) or a Redshank (lower right) may be seen moving from stone to stone, scanning the water for edibles.

Further downstream a heron stands on the grassy bank watching for any unsuspecting fish.

For much of the year the colourful Grey Wagtail, belying its name with its bright yellow underneath, hunts for flies along the water's edge, so I'll close this chapter with a Grey Wagtail by the River Derwent. There's be more to say about Wagtails on pages 79 and 80.

2.

The Birds I See Most

Before looking more broadly at the various categories of birds I come across during my walks, in the next three sections I'll show some pictures and say something about the species that I see most frequently. In fact it is fair to say that not to meet these each day is unusual for most of the year, wherever my walks take me in this area.

Oystercatchers
Cormorants
Grey Herons

I could also include Gulls, Crows, Mallards, Blackbirds, Starlings, Greylag Geese and Swans in this section but will come to them eventually.

Oystercatcher (*Haematopus ostralegus*)

Of all the Waders these are the ones that year round I see most often on this particular stretch of coastline, although at some times of year Redshanks outnumber them. From January to December it is rare for me to take a walk by the harbour or the sea without seeing several.

Their bold black and white outline and bright orange-red bill make an Oystercatcher stand out prominently at a distance even against dark backgrounds such as this seaweed opposite the port.

During the summer breeding season they are often in grassy areas. Here is one that has caught a worm on the grass of the landscaped slag bank by the Workington shore. In 2021 a pair raised two chicks on a pebble bank by the River Derwent, and were often seen feeding on the grass of the nearby Mill Field.

A more popular Oystercatcher meal, though, is crab caught at to the edge of the tide, and what's better than rooting in the seaweed and sand on the estuary. Yes, Oystercatchers are primarily birds of the coast, and they love the mud as the tide recedes, but they're flexible. I've photographed them in a wide variety of settings but their main environment is as in the image below, at Flimby shore.

It doesn't take a lot to frighten Oystercatchers into flying noisily away and when one goes they usually all go. These were part of a flock of about thirty.

Here is possibly my best photo of an Oystercatcher, and interestingly it has a yellowish end to its bill. Most others that I have seen are totally bright orange-red.

I mentioned the pair that in 2021 bred on the pebbly island just downstream of the Yearl weir. I was able to follow them from their mating through to chick care. Copulation was frequent over several weeks but unlike what I have seen with gulls and herons there was never any trace of bonding "affection". It seemed mechanical. Anyway, eggs were laid, three hatched and at least one survived

There were two for quite a while but then the last time I saw them, only one seemed to be still there. The island by the Yearl is dangerous territory for chicks. Just across the river is a heronry, and their chicks are hungry. Herons have to eat too.

Cormorant (*Phalacrocorax carbo*)

From by the River Trent in the East Midlands I had been familiar with Cormorants. Or so I thought. Nothing had prepared me for the vision of hundreds of these large black birds crammed during a winter high tide onto the jetty by the Port of Workington. This below was a relatively modest number one February day.

I understand that up to 1200 birds have been counted at times in the past. My own highest count (very approximate, I must add) is 900. Cormorants are migratory birds and in Winter the waters of the Derwent estuary by the Solway provide for some a stopping off point for feeding and rest en route to somewhere further south, whilst for others this is an attractive spot in which to stay and spend the colder months with a plentiful supply of food. Some may in fact be resident all year round, but I have not been able to trace any systematic research on this.

This short chapter is to introduce birds that I see very often in many different places, and I should say that the Derwent estuary is far from the only place to see Cormorants. They're to be found all up and down the coast, often standing with

wings spread out to dry. On this day it may have been dull drizzly damp but still after some swimming and diving this Cormorant, now standing alone by the estuary channel at Anthorn, needed to dry his feathers. Unlike many other diving birds the Cormorant's feathers are not well waterproofed with oils. They need to take care of them in this way.

And here's one in the old Workington harbour. He's had a successful dive. Cormorants are skilled fish catchers. I don't understand the details but it seems that the reason for the numbers congregating on the Derwent estuary is a good supply of the fish they need to survive winter to breed again another year.

Grey Heron (*Ardea cinerea*)

Of the places where I walk, only in woodlands am I unlikely to see a Heron, and they're there as well if there is water around. By the river bank, at the shore and harbours, and by the ponds, herons are stand in the shallows waiting for unsuspecting fish.

By the pond one can often see several herons partially hidden in the reeds. A hungry heron can take a sizeable fish, rodent or bird, even up to a small duck and certainly ducklings in the season. I recall an entire brood of eight Mallard ducklings being wiped out within forty-eight hours. It's sad, and yet the Heron chicks have to be fed.

Above an adult heron flies low over the water at the Siddick Pond. This bird on the right, is fishing in the light of the warm evening sun. An inexperienced young bird, I think, as it appears to be fishing in an unlikely spot.

Photographing birds at their nests can be very disruptive to their lives, and under normal circumstances I avoid it. However, this Heron pair and their nest could easily be seen from a well-used public pathway and they didn't appear to be at all troubled by that fact. With my 600 mm zoom lens I was able to get these photos.

My favourite photo from 2021: **"Heron among the Lilies"**

3.

Back to the Shoreline

Waders

In my introductory pages I referred briefly to several Waders (or Shorebirds as Americans call them) and followed it up with some pages about Oystercatchers. Now it's time to look at a number of other species in this group that I see on a more or less frequent basis.

Curlew (*Numenius arquata*)

The Curlew, or to give its fuller name the Eurasian Curlew, is the largest of the waders that we see along coast and is easily recognised by its distinctive long, smoothly downward curving bill. Sadly, what was a common sight is now less so, and the Curlew is now viewed nationally as an endangered species..

Despite the numbers dropping rapidly in recent years, I have found that along the West Cumbria coast individual birds are regularly seen feeding at the edge of the tide. This photo was taken by the Derwent estuary at Workington, just opposite the entrance to the port, one of my regular spots for "wader-hunting" as well as looking for Mediterranean Gulls. If you know where to look there are often small flocks to be photographed. A favourite spot for me is on the shore between the sewage works and Flimby, which is where this next photo was taken.

On this day there was a Curlew flock of around a hundred lined along the margin of the water. Several times they spotted me before I could get photographs and the nearer birds flew a short distance along the shore to get away from me.. At last I managed to crawl up the dune, poke my long lens through some tall grass and take several shots before they spotted the movement and were off again. There were probably a few Whimbrel there among them (smaller, shorter bill and striped head) but I've never confidently identified a Whimbrel locally.

Lapwing (*Vanellus vanellus*)

The Northern Lapwing has several other names, Peewit and Green Plover among them. I've seen them all the way along the West Cumbria coast, but the largest numbers have been at Anthorn, huge flocks pushed onto the sand banks by the tide and accompanied by sometimes even greater numbers of Golden Plovers.

This Lapwing was patrolling the water's edge at Bowness on Solway in September 2020, close to the northerly limit of my range for this book. Occasionally a small flock, or sometimes just an individual, can be seen by the pond at Siddick reserve.

This group was part of a much larger flock at Anthorn late on a January afternoon in 2022. There's little colour to be seen as the light was fading. As is often the case there were Lapwings and Golden Plovers together. Frequently they form almost parallel lines, the Lapwings closer to the water and the Golden Plovers behind.

Although I've usually seen and photographed them by the water, Lapwings are also often to be found on grassland, both when the incoming tide has driven them inland, and also during the breeding season. This proud looking bird was standing in the middle of a field at the Campfield Marsh RSPB reserve one early afternoon in April 2022. The staff there were feeling very pleased at the number of breeding Lapwing pairs. Although in the winter there can be well over half a million Lapwing in Britain due to influxes from the continent, and over 100,000 pairs breed here each year the numbers are in significant decline.

Oystercatcher (*Haematopus ostralegus*)

I already included the Oystercatcher as one of the birds that I most commonly see, whether at the river, the pond or the seashore for much of the year. However, simply because it is one of my favourite subjects I can't resist adding another image here here in the alphabetical sequence of waders..

This was one of my very first Oystercatcher photos, and also one of my first photos of any bird using what was then my new 600 mm zoom lens. These two were at the most northerly end of my "West Cumbria" range, Bowness-on-Solway,

For about fifteen minutes I watched this parent and youngster far away on the sand but brought close by the zoom. I wonder what was going on between the two of them. It rather looks like a telling-off for some minor misdemeanour. I see myself primarily as a budding bird photographer not as a bird watcher, but watching bird behaviour can be quite fascinating.

Redshank (*Tringa totanus*)

These smaller birds share one feature with Oystercatchers. They are noisy creatures. Vary easily scared, they fly away at the slightest warning of human presence. Apparently they're known as "the guardians of the marshes" because of their sensitivity to potential predators.

Taking photos through a long lens is not difficult but I find it a challenge to get very close to a Redshank.

The photograph above is from an August afternoon near Allonby, the birds standing clear of the incoming tide. I also have photos of them on the pebbles at the edge of the River Derwent a miler or two upstream from the port. However, apart from during the breeding season, when they're away in the hills, the best places in the area that I've found to see Redshanks in substantial numbers, are on the low-tide mud banks in the harbours at Maryport and Harrington.

Workington tends not to have so many, and I'm not sure about Whitehaven, but clearly there's something they like about the Maryport and Harrington mud and what they can find in it.

Ringed Plover (*Charadrius hiaticula*)

The Ringed Plover is to be found up and down the coast, usually in quite small numbers but occasionally as sizeable flocks. I've already shown several photos in the chapter "Where I Walk".

Sometimes in the early days I would refer to "a little Ringed Plover", meaning simply that the Ringed Plover is quite a small bird. However, this tended to cause confusion as the Ringed Plover (Charadrius hiaticula) has a smaller cousin known as the "Little Ringed Plover"(Charadrius dubius) which is quite rare in Cumbria and I've never seen one here although many in Somerset and Norfolk.

> Incidentally, all the photos on this and the facing page were taken with my old Nikon D3000 camera and 300 mm zoom lens, proving once again (a point I know I'm making repeatedly) that you don't need the latest expensive kit to produce acceptable images.

I quite often see Ringed Plovers and Turnstones together at the edge of tide as in this image, usually with the larger and stronger Turnstones closer to the waves.

The first time I saw a flock of Ringed Plover was back in September 2020 on the pebbles at the north end of the Old Side shore at Workington, and above is all that could be seen. The camouflage was amazing, then:

Turnstone (*Arenaria interpres*)

This also is a bird that I've mentioned several times already. I've heard some people refer to them as timid birds that fly away at the slightest sign of a human, but that isn't my experience of them and it has often been possible to get quite close up even with my limited fieldcraft skills.

The bird to the left here, at Silloth in October 2022, is in its winter plumage. The one below, taken at Silloth on what was only my second local outing with the camera looking for birds by the sea, back in August 2020, shows a small flock of Turnstones, many in full Summer breeding colour.

The first bird was also one of a small flock. I'd been waiting to meet a friend by the Silloth promenade when I noticed people pointing cameras at something over the sea wall. Being inquisitive I went to take a look.

The tide was well in, and a flock of Turnstones had taken refuge from the deepening water, perching on the seaweed-covered breakwater, or what bit of it was still not under water. I couldn't resist going back to the car from my camera (not the long lens but a more carryable 400 mm zoom). The pictures opposite tell the story. I crept up closer and thought I was doing well, but it takes just one bird to start an evacuation.

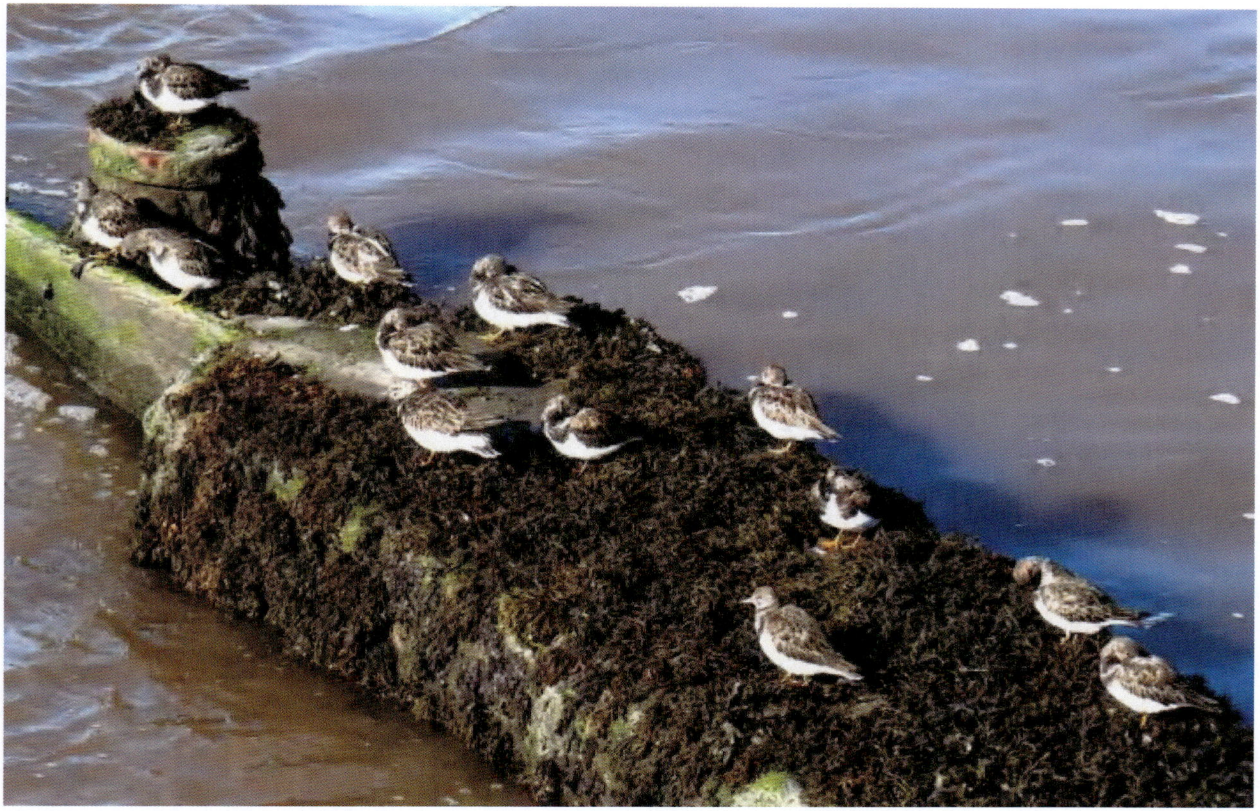

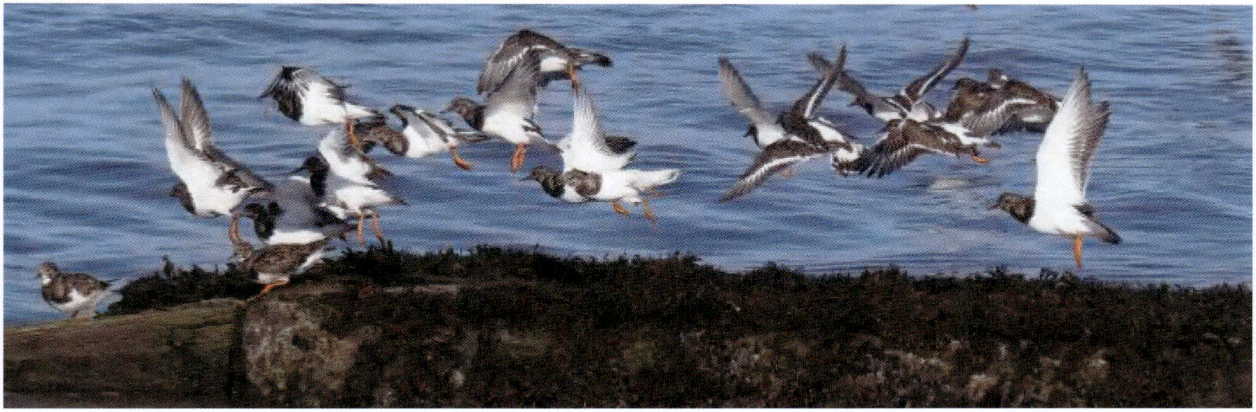

Some Other Waders I've Seen Occasionally

All the birds in this Waders section so far are species that I see frequently apart from when they disappear to their breeding grounds, but then they reappear later in the summer or early autumn. The following, though, are birds which I've seen occasionally, mostly as they're passing through on their annual migratory journey.

First a **Dunlin**, feeding by the River Derwent estuary at Workington. I've only seen one or two very occasionally. This one was here at the end of April 2022, probably on its way north to Iceland, having spent the winter in Africa. It's a small Sandpiper with a black, slightly down-curved bill, and notice the black patch on the belly.

The next is not a good photo, and I'm only including it because it's the only one I have of **Knot**, another Sandpiper species larger than the Dunlin. It was taken in July 2022 at almost the same spot as the one of the Dunlin, but in very different lighting conditions. These are not especially rare, but whereas they're seen in their thousands on Morecambe Bay they're less common on the Solway coast, and I understand not often seen here in July. They pass through on their way to and from Canada and Greenland.

And now a third not so common Sandpiper, often at Workington as a winter visitor after spending summer in Greenland. The **Purple Sandpiper** (Calidris maritima) from November through to January is often seen on rocks at the end of the breakwater by the old coastguard lookout. From my point of view the problem is getting to a place from which to see them. In one's late-70s, with balance not as good as it once was, it's wise to wait for a day when the surface of the pier is dry. However, here (right) is a shot from December 2021.

And finally, a larger bird that I've now seen several times on the shore at Flimby during its migratory season. The **Bar-Tailed Godwit**. They spend summers in Siberia, and in early May, would be on their way north. There's a related Black-tailed Godwit too, which I've never managed to photograph successfully near home, but one damp mid-May afternoon near the Campfield Marsh RSPB entrance I parked in a layby. If it hadn't been for a young lady parking next to me and pointing them out, I would surely have missed the **Black-tailed Godwit** flock in the distance. I waited for a lull in the rain and got the shot below (600 mm zoom lens). Being May the birds were in their breeding colours; non-breeding plumage is much plainer. You might also (or might not) be able to see the slightly upturned bills compared with their Bar-tailed cousins.

> If only the weather had been better, but that's bird photography hobby for you. If you can wait days for the perfect conditions, fine, but then probably the birds won't be there. You've got to go with what you've got and do your best with the challenges of distance, dim light and drizzle then see what a bit of digital image processing can do.

4.

Birds in the Bushes

Perching Birds, the Passerines

The title of this section could well include trees, reeds and grass, but for brevity I'm leaving it as bushes. These are the birds that are less likely to be seen at the edge of the tide or on the pond than perching on and among vegetation of many kinds - although some, such as Dippers, Wagtails and Wrens enjoy the riverbank. To include all the passerines seen in this area would make this a much larger book, so this chapter contains just a small selection.

If I'd been able to include shots of hirundines feeding in the air this is where I would have put them, but unfortunately all my attempts to get usable photos of swallows, swifts and martins have been abject failures. They move so fast! Maybe next year.

Blackbird (*Turdus merula*)

One of my early memories involving a Blackbird is of being ill in bed as a child and being woken at some ridiculous hour each morning by one singing right outside my bedroom window when all I wanted to do was sleep. At that time I could happily have shot it, and not with a camera.

Of course, down the years my attitude to this elegant bird has matured and it is good to see them both in the trees and on the ground, sometimes busily occupied searching for food, and at others singing enthusiastically from a high branch like the one in the photo above, by the Siddick Pond.

Although an adult male Blackbird is indeed black, or mostly so, females and juveniles are brown. I haven't done a careful count but of all the perching birds this is one of most commonly seen in the areas where I walk, following closely after Chaffinch, Great Tit and Dunnock.

On the Mill Field, early one May morning, the dew still on the grass this early bird has caught the worm.

This photo is from January 2022 and I originally had it labelled on Facebook as a female Blackbird. Now I've been told that, although a female would be similarly brown, there are four colour differences that I should have picked up: the head, the throat, the bill and the tail. Seemingly it's a male in its first winter. Come summer it will be back.

There's so much to learn, and to be honest at my age it doesn't all stick in the mind when first learned.

Blue Tit (*Cyanistes caeruleus*)

Continuing down my steadily expanding list of birds seen and "shot" we come to the Blue Tit, but I'll deviate from a strict alphabetical order because it doesn't seem sensible to separate the different species of Tit.

My experience of the small reserve at Crosscannonby Scar over the past two or three years has been one of feast or famine, but on this April afternoon in 2021 there was definitely a feast. This Blue Tit was sitting watching the world go by as I was following the antics of a Chiffchaff, We'll see the latter shortly, but here I must comment on something that I missed at the time. I had not noticed the ring. I can't see anything meaningful on it, but if by some miracle someone connected with a Blue Tit ringing project happens to see this then maybe it will tell them something. And now, moving forward nine months, another ringed Blue Tit, this time right at the inland boundary of what I've defined as my territory for this book, at Mockerkin Tarn near the road towards Loweswater. It was a bitterly cold mid-January morning but this little bird never gave up hunting for whatever few edible morsels might be there to find.

Below: April by the cycle path at Siddick Pond. I like the way the foliage acts as camouflage for the Blue Tit.

Coal Tit (*Periparus ater*)

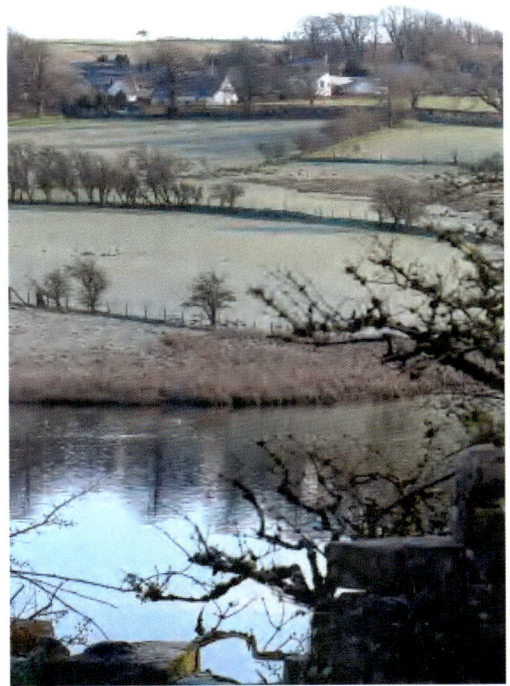

One of my Blue Tit photos having been taken by Mockerkin Tarn I thought I'd show a picture of one end of the tarn as the next two bird photos come from the same spot in January 2022.

This is my only local West Cumbria photo of a Coal Tit. Is this because the Coal Tit is rare around here? According to the Cumbria Bird Club annual publication it is an "abundant resident" so I must just be missing them..

Two other tits that I've never seen are the Marsh Tit (mostly in the south of the county) and the Willow Tit (mostly in the north), but after mentioning what I haven't seen, here at last is my Coal Tit.

It's a pity about the twig cutting him in two . I only saw him briefly. Once again there's a leg ring that I didn't notice at the time. Nowadays I'd be taking shot after shot in an attempt to get a readable image and report it to the project.

The next two photos are without any text. The Great Tit, also a ringed bird although hidden in this image, is from Mockerkin. The Long-tailed Tit is from Siddick Pond.

Great Tit (*Parus major*)

Long-tailed Tit (*Aegithalos caudatus*)

Bullfinch (*Pyrrhula pyrrhula*)

It was the end of a May afternoon in 2021. My cousin Dorothy and I were walking along the path by the Siddick Pond when she suddenly caught hold of my arm to stop me and whispered, "There's a Bullfinch". I could see that she was pointing along the path to the grass verge but my problem was that I didn't know what I was looking for. I'd never knowingly seen a Bullfinch before. Then suddenly, there it was. I've seen many since then; they are spectacular birds when in full colour, the male as usual being the brighter.

Reed Bunting (*Emberiza schoeniclus*)

The two Buntings that I've photographed so far were seen in very different environments. The one on this page, a **Reed Bunting** was perched among the reeds at Siddick Pond whereas the other, a Snow Bunting (on the back cover), was moving around among the pebbles on the shore near the old coastguard lookout.

In my experience at least, to get a decent photograph of a Reed Bunting demands patience. I've stood with camera and long lens for lengthy periods by those reeds, seeing the birds in the distance flit from place to place, periodically clicking the shutter only to find that what I thought was a nicely perched bird had turned its back on me or was largely masked by inconveniently place stalks. This is my best so far, a long-distance shot. I'm quite please with it but will keep trying.

Chaffinch (*Fringilla coelebs*)

I think this was the first photograph that I took of a Chaffinch, back in 2020 At least it's the first one that I knew to be a Chaffinch. I'm afraid, though, that I can't claim to have known that when I pressed the shutter button. It was only after asking online that I was told "Female Chaff."

Like the Bullfinch the male Chaffinch is the more colourful, more visible, more photogenic. I've probably "shot" more male Chaffinches than any other perching bird, and I guess that's not really surprising as the Chaffinch is one of our most common British birds. There are said to be something like 6 million resident pairs in Great Britain and another 2 million in Ireland.

Although not so tame as many a Robin they will often "pose" rather than fly away at the first sight of a human. This bird in March 2021 stayed perched high on his branch by the Pond for a long time, allowing me to photograph him from several angles and distances.

I was about to write that they can be "noisy" birds, but that might seem to have negative connotations. I like the sound of a Chaffinch singing with enthusiasm from a high branch in Spring.

Chiffchaff (*Phylloscopus collybita*)

This little warbler is a bird that I see frequently in many places, and even more often hear from inside the trees and bushes by the path. Due to my hearing difficulties I'm not good at recognising birdsong, but the Chiffchaff is so distinctive that it's difficult to mistake. "Chiff-chaff-chiff-chaff-chiff-chaff". So goes the song, unlike any other bird.

The problem with identification arises when the bird is not singing. Then it looks almost the same as a Willow Warbler. Of course, experienced bird watchers will say, No, there are several differences between the two. Well, yes, there are but to a newcomer they're often (usually, in my experience) not massive enough to be certain. However, this one has been confirmed by others who know better, and to be absolutely honest I'd be happy with the photo even if it did turn out to be a Willow Warbler. (Do I hear gasps of ornithological astonishment?)

There were several Chiffchaffs around in the woods at Crosscannony Scar on that April day and here's another one, busily flitting from tree to tree. It has something in its bill, but I can't tell what.

Dunnock (*Prunella modularis*)

The Dunnock is often looked down on as an insignificant bird. Its old name name was "Hedge Sparrow", but it definitely is no sparrow. Sparrows are finches, with the finch style of bill. See the House Sparrow opposite or the Chaffinch a page or two back.

This first photograph was taken in May 2022 as I walking along the path to the shore near Flimby in hope of finding some waders. In front of me was a large bush with dark green depths, but sitting just outside the shadow was this little Dunnock. The Curlews and Oystercatchers could wait for a few minutes while I paid attention to this little bird.

Almost exactly a year earlier this Dunnock had posed for me by the cycle path near Siddick Pond. Very often as I walk along that path I see several Dunnocks hopping around on the path itself and the grass at the side. Catch one in the right light and their rich colouring is beautiful.

House Sparrow (*Passer domesticus*)

The House Sparrow surely needs little introduction, although I must say that I've never photographed one near the house. Here are two from bushes by the cycle path.

People still talk of going "up the line" because this used to be the railway track between Workington and the mines around the Cleator area, above Whitehaven. The progenitors of these sparrows were probably little phased by the passing engines and trucks of past decades, and now tolerate the passing humans, even those with cameras.

The bird at the top is a male, while the lower one is a female.

54

Goldfinch (*Carduelis carduelis*)

I wonder how many times I've written earlier in this book that it's the male that has the bright colouring, the female being much more subdued in appearance. Well, with a Goldfinch it isn't true. Both male and female share the colours. According to one of my books distinguishing between them is somewhere between difficult and impossible, although they must be able to tell the difference.

Over the past two or three years I've taken many photographs of birds in full song, Blackbirds, Chiffchaffs and Chaffinches especially but looking through my Goldfinch shots this one, against a pale sky is the only one I can find of a Goldfinch.

These are common resident birds throughout Great Britain except for the most northerly tips. In West Cumbria I've seen them in just about every area that I've walked including even finding them perched on pebbles by the shore, although the photos came out very blurry. They're beautiful birds, a joy to see and joy to capture in the camera.

Without any hesitation I can say that this is my favourite Goldfinch photograph. In the bushes beside the cycle track close to the Igesund factory I spotted the adult and pointed my lens. I had not noticed the chick until I looked at the camera screen afterwards and almost fell over with surprise. I'd caught the adult feeding the chick, the kind of shot that I couldn't have dreamed of.

And that's the way it goes. Frequent disappointments when I think I've got it right, but then compensation for them all when suddenly something like this happens.

Stonechat (*Saxicola rubicola*)

When I walk, as I often do on a Summer evening, along the patch by the Derwent estuary opposite the Port of Workington the bird I most often find (and it's rare for them to be missing) is the Stonechat. Here's my friend, "Mr. Stonechat" who willingly poses just a few feet from the path.

"Mrs. Stonechat" was often around too but I never got a really good picture of her. However, here, in late August, is a juvenile. In 2022 they raised at least two, and I think three, broods in a patch of dense bushes so this would be one of their youngsters from earlier in the year.

Sedge Warbler
(*Acrocephalus Schoenobaenus*)

Earlier I said that, in my experience so far, getting a good shot of a Reed Bunting demanded a lot of patience. I'd been told that there was a Sedge Warbler in the reeds by the Pond, very close to where a month later I would be watching for the Bunting.

Patience yet again, not this time because of the bird constantly moving around but rather because its rarely showed itself at all. However, when it deigned to make an appearance it stayed around for about ten minutes, occasionally moving from stalk to stalk before settling on one of them. This photo was the upshot.

It's a small bird, only seen at a distance that April morning in 2021. I've never seen one since even though according to the statistics they're not rare and I'm told there were five pairs in that area.

It's a great memory, all the better for the fact that the bird was singing.

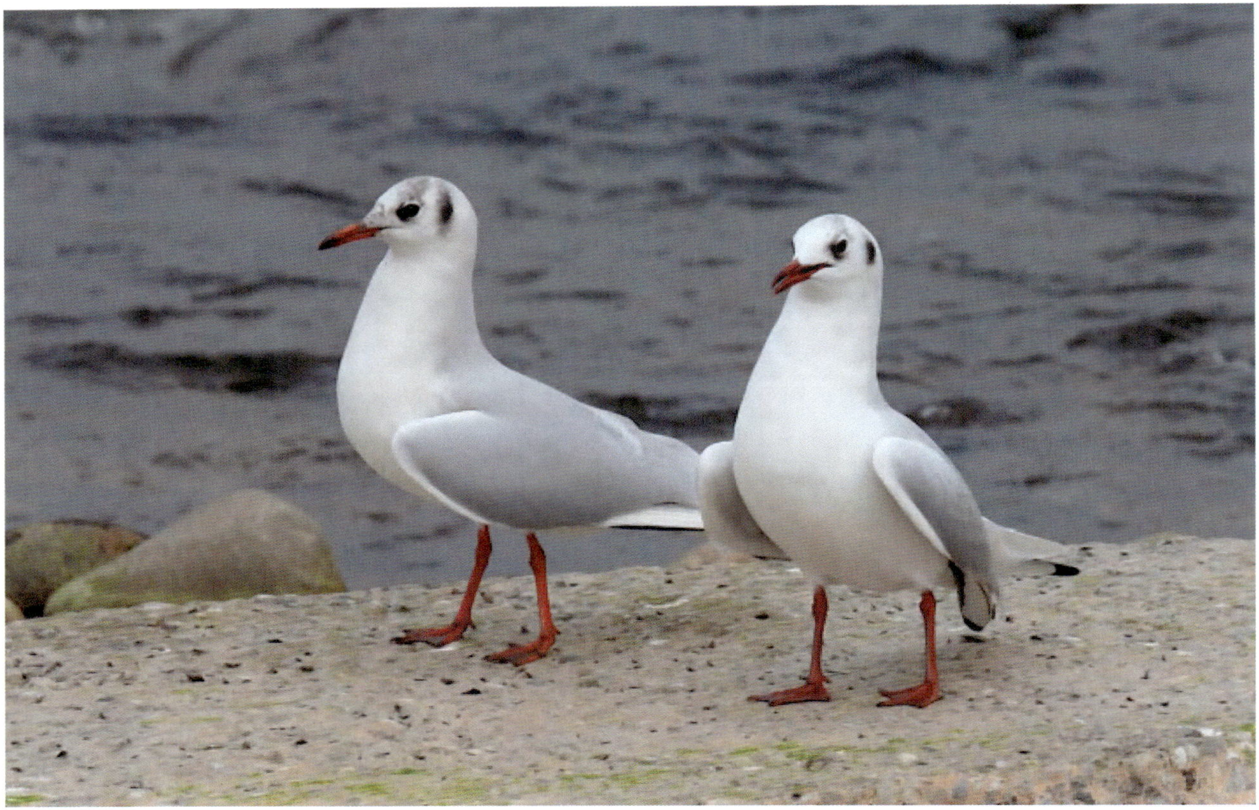

5.

A Little Larology - Gulls

It is no exaggeration to say that for many people gulls are far from being their favourite birds. My own memories of them are certainly not all positive. I recall, for example, the day when with my wife I was sitting eating a sandwich lunch by the harbour at Conwy in North Wales and suddenly her sandwich disappeared from her hand as a streak of white feathers passed in front of her. To say the least she was not pleased.

Having said that, however, there are enthusiastic larologists (those who study gulls - from Latin, *larus*) who can only be described as larophiles (lovers of gulls) and without doubt Gulls can be very interesting. What surprised me on living by the sea for the first time since I was seven years old was the variety of species and the multiple stages of their life-cycles.

I'll not in the following pages be going into all of that but will show, for each of the gull species that I have seen in this area, a few photos to illustrate the variety.

Herring Gull (*Larus argentatus*)

Talk about a "seagull" to any gull enthusiast and you're likely to be told in no uncertain terms, "There's no such bird".

In strictly ornithological terms that is certainly true, but in common parlance the mature Herring Gull is what we usually mean. Here's one in its summer feathers and at least five years old. It will have gone through several stages of appearance to reach this. The picture below is of a parent and gull chick on the shore at Maryport one August afternoon in 2020, one of the first photos I took with my new camera and long lens. It was completely unplanned, purely opportunistic as I was walking along the promenade and spotted this gull chick pestering its harassed mother for food. The youngster scarcely looks like a gull, and, assuming it survives will change its plumage twice a year for four or five years before becoming an adult.

On this page I'll show two more Herring Gull shots to illustrate different aspects of their lives. Above, this adult has caught a crab at Silloth so it won't need to steal people's chips today. Finally this one was flying over Siddick Pond very purposefully. No gliding around in circles today. This was a straight line flight toward a destination.

Lesser Black-Backed Gull (*Larus fuscus*)

Among the Herring Gulls typically seen at the seaside there will usually be a few Lesser Black-backed Gulls.

These, as shown in the picture of the pair here, have a much darker grey back than the Herring Gull. In fact, depending on the light, they can look totally black.

An adult with its bright, clean, orange-yellow legs (as distinct from the pink of the Herring Gull) is an handsome bird, not much different in size from the Herring Gull; slightly smaller but the size ranges overlap.

Great Black-Backed Gull (*Larus marinus*)

Before moving on to the smaller gull we must look at the largest of all, the Great Black-backed Gull. This is a monster, a powerful bird with a massive bill. Compared with the Lesser Black-backed it is larger, blacker and has pink rather than yellow legs. Its wingspan can be over 1.6 metres.

The group photo above, shot at a great distance from Maryport promenade, illustrates the difference in size of a Great Black-backed Gull against the surrounding Herring Gulls whilst the one below shows that it has the strength to take and carry sizeable fish from the water. I've seen one tackle more than this but didn't get a photo.

Black-Headed Gull (*Chroicocephalus ridibundus*)

We now move to a smaller bird, the Black-Headed Gull. As the pictures here show it's appearance in the Spring/Summer breeding season is very different from the Winter. The breeding season "black" heads are in fact a chocolate brown, but in most lights look to be black. The left-hand image, from Harrington harbour in July 2021, shows it well. Outside the breading season the head becomes white apart from a black dot behind the eye as in the right-hand picture from Workington Mill Field, December 2021. He was the noisy one of a small flock, then flew away.

Other Smaller Gulls

To show all the different stages of development of immature gulls from their juvenile plumage through to adulthood would take more space than I have in this book. Also, I don't consider myself competent to do it. I get the ageing of gulls wrong so often that I could lead you far astray. Having said that, I do enjoy trying to capture the various stages for each species in my camera, so maybe one day …

Meanwhile here are two other species, less often seen than those already shown On the left is a **Mediterranean Gull (*Larus melanocephalus*)** - it may be the whitest gull; the grey is very pale. In Summer this also has a black head. On the right is a **Common Gull (*Larus canus*)**. It's name suggests that they're everywhere, but that isn't so in this area. Note the rounded head, gentler appearance and greyish legs.

These two were at the same spot on the same grey October day, both in winter plumage. Mediterranean and Black-headed Gulls are often there together, with the occasional Common Gull in the mixture, smaller gulls together.

Mediterranean Gull flying up the Derwent estuary, Workington, August 2022

6.

At the Pond: Ducks, Geese, Swans and More

Ducks, geese and a wide variety of water birds are to be seen at the local ponds, the major area from my point of view being the Siddick Ponds nature reserve. We've already looked at some of the birds regularly seen here, the Cormorant and Grey Heron. It's not unusual, either, to see a Little Egret; in fact on one occasion I saw four of them together, and sometimes a Heron and a Little Egret can be seen fishing side by side in the margins of a reed bed. But now we'll look at some of the other birds, those actually on the water rather than by its side.

Coot (*Fulica atra*) and Moorhen (*Gallinula chloropus*)

I thought I would show these on the same page. One or two people have asked me how to tell the difference between them. When seen separately there may appear to be similarities but side by side the differences are clear.

At Siddick Pond on a grey February morning the white bills and faces of this Coot pair stand out. It's quite usual to see ten or twelve Coots there, but occasionally during the migration season there are much larger flocks.

At Mockerkin Tarn on an exceptionally cold January day this Moorhen was navigating the area not covered by ice. Red bill and white on the side.

The image below is from above the Yearl weir on the River Derwent. This poor bird once had a nice home.

"The Morning After The Flood" - A Moorhen surveys the wreckage. Where's my nest?

A Variety of Ducks

On Siddick Pond in particular there is such a variety of ducks throughout the year. I can only show a few here. Others include Tufted Duck, Teal, Widgeon, Pochard and many more.

There is usually at least one **Mallard (*Anas platyrhynchos*)** pair by the Yearl weir. For this photo I've stretched the definition of pond. Above the weir there is a pond-like area. Mallards are noted for being promiscuous and polygamous. Quite often a male will have several females in tow.

This male **Goldeneye (*Bucephala clangula*)** was on the Siddick Pond. Numbers are rarely large but there are often some here outside their breeding season, for which they mostly migrate to Scandinavia. They're diving ducks which disappear under water and you've to watch carefully to see where they surface.

The male **Shoveler (*Anas clypeata*)** here is another winter visitor. A few breed in the UK, but almost certainly this one will have flown in from Iceland for the winter. For many Siddick Pond is a rest stop on the way south but this is a January photo so he may have been staying until time to return north.

Greylag Geese (*Anser anser*)

Siddick Pond is a popular spot with Greylag Geese. They're resident all year around and breed, with usually several families of goslings each Spring, good numbers of which survive.

Combined family outing. Quite often there's more than one family together. So far as I could tell there were two families here, but six adults. Why the other two adults, I wonder. Could they be young adults that haven't bred this year but join in the collective child care?

Goosander (*Mergus merganser*)

The female can look sleek and also can seem to be having a "bad hair day". The male's appearance is very different, black and white in the breeding season, but goes into eclipse plumage in the summer, also red-headed.

Below is a Goosander mother and family at the River Derwent, by the Mill Field, Workington in July 2022.

Female Goosander
Early morning light against the mist of the raging weir

Swans

Around the year we see **Mute Swans (*Cygnus olor*)** at many places in the area. Occasionally these are joined by one or more **Whooper Swans (*Cygnus cygnus*)**. In this image the two are show together, Mute Swan in front.

Opposite is a Black Swan. This is native to Australia and many birders will not record its presence because it is not indigenous to Britain and will sometimes claim that they are all escapees from bird collections.. However, they are now quite widely spread around the country and are known to to have bred in some areas.

Maybe I'm demonstrating that I'm not "a true birder" by including this foreign species. But I don't care; it's a beautiful bird. In fact it's the only one that I have pursued day after day until I got a photo. After hearing that a **Black Swan (*Cygnus atratus*)** had arrived on migration it took me six visits to Siddick Pond before it eventually showed itself while I was there. Many migrants rest and feed for a day, then at night they're off on the next stage of their journeys. Fortunately, unlike many, this bird decided to stay for a while. Oops! Maybe I'm becoming a twitcher after all.

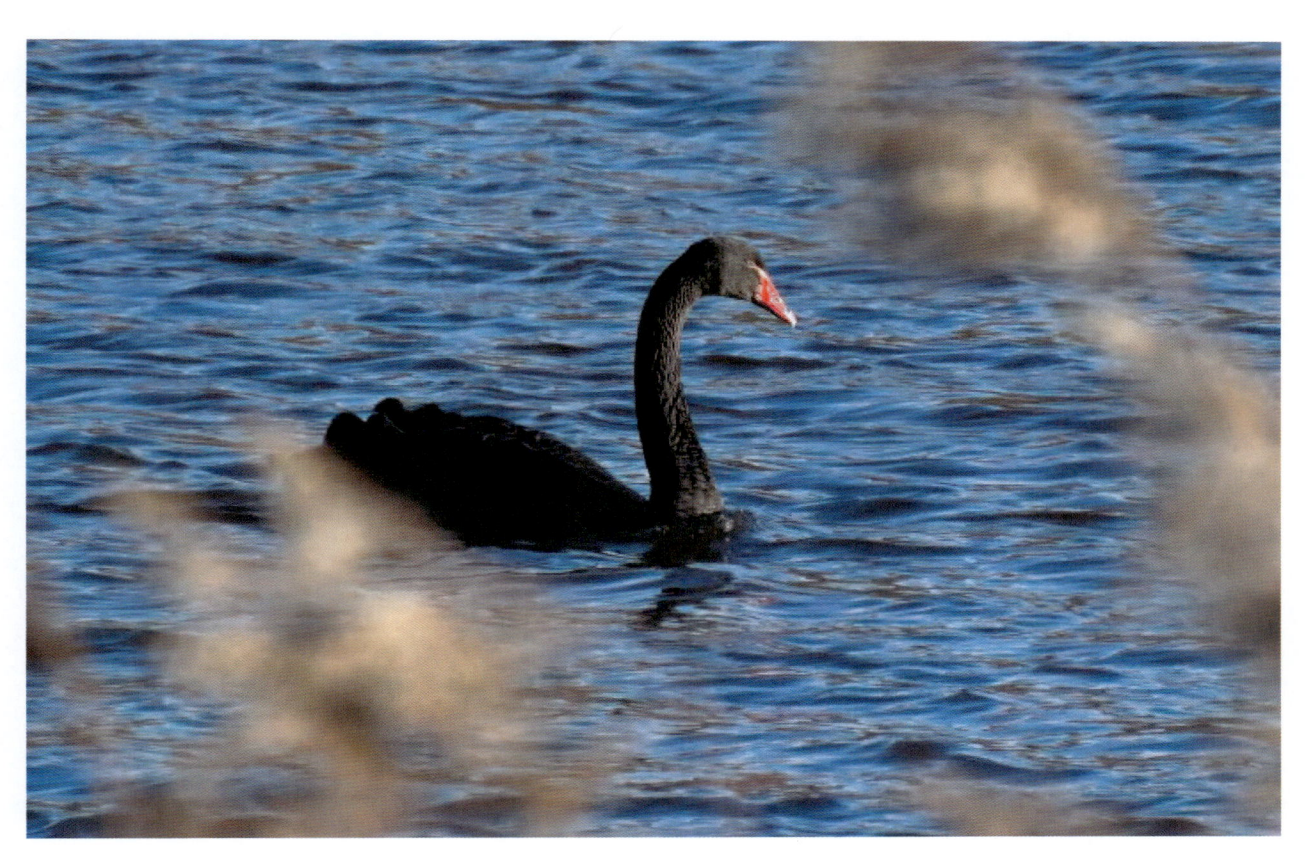

Swan conference on a cold morning at Siddick Pond
Can't you hear them saying, "We should complain! Who turned the central heating off?"

7.

Birds by the River and Stream

Many of the birds commonly seen by the River Derwent have already been discussed in the chapter on birds at the pond, so I'll not duplicate. Mallards, Goosanders, Swans, Little Grebes are all frequently to be seen either below or above the Yearl weir. Herons abound, Little Egrets are becoming increasingly common, and of course Gulls and Corvids are everywhere. Kingfishers are often around, but I've never managed to get a photo. Here we'll look at just five birds, shown in this chapter simply because by the river or the nearby stream is where I usually see them, although not all the photos are from the riverside.

Pied Wagtail (*Motacilla alba yarrellii*)

I've seen these by the riverside, at the pond, on the shore, and especially on the car park where they dodge between the moving cars. The bird on the right I saw in September 2020 just past the end of Maryport promenade, the first time I walked its length. The juvenile below was by the edge of the smaller Siddick Pond in August 2022.

Grey Wagtail (*Motacilla cinerea*)

I've lost count of the number of times someone has told me, while walking with my camera alongside the River Derwent in Workington's Mill Field, "There's a Yellow Wagtail just a bit further along". What they've seen has been a Grey Wagtail. Yes, its underparts may be bright yellow but its back is grey. This is not to say that Yellow Wagtails are never seen in Cumbria. They are, but as very much a rarity, and certainly so in the west. These two should illustrate the point about colour.

It's great to watch them flit from stone to stone early on a Spring morning, collecting insects, then vanishing, only to return for another batch of food to take to the nest. Many a time I've gone out for an hour only to discover that two have passed, or even three, while "shooting" these and our next bird.

Dipper (*Cinclus cinclus*)

I love watching a Dipper dive from a rock into the current of the River Derwent and emerge further downstream. I fact I like them so much that I'm giving them a double page and big images.

Often the Dipper is seen in photographs, including mine, as a rather dumpy little bird, but that's just a matter of posture. Here, with neck outstretched, he's observing the stream with meticulous care. After all, there's food down there if only it can be caught.

This Dipper is skipping across the pebbles by the River Derwent towards the stream. It look as though it's been hunting insects for a while as an alternative to diving in the water. Wet or dry, it's food.

The bird in the lower picture was on the bank of the River Cocker in the park at Cockermouth and has just succeeded in catching something from the water. Later I saw the same bird with a bill full of insects.

From a photographic point of view getting the lower image was difficult due to the dim light down by the water's edge. The upper one was easy.

Wren (*Troglodytes troglodytes*)

This little bird is found in many different settings. My Wren photographs range from trees and shrubs to streams and swamps. Simply because the first time I ever managed to get a recognisable photo of a Wren was by a stream I decided to put it in this section.

And here it is, not the best image in the world but my first of a Wren, rummaging around among the undergrowth on the muddy bank of the stream in the Harrington reserve.

My next was also by a stream, this time a feeder stream of the River Derwent by the Mill Field. This one actually made me think that my fieldcraft might be improving as I achieved the shot by creeping up slowly and quietly, but pride comes before a fall and since then I've as often as not succeeded in frightening birds away when trying to get closer. They say that practice makes perfect. Well, I've a lot more practising to do.

The more I do this bird photography the more I realise the complexities of it. At first it's a matter of point and click, and sometimes a decent image materialises, especially if the light is good. But "shooting" birds in their natural home environments often involves dim light and difficult-to-reach places. It's a challenge, especially as one's view of what is an acceptable image is enhanced by experience.

Having shown two difficult Wren images I'll finish up with one that was much easier because the light was good and the bird was standing still, at least for a few seconds, then when it moved it didn't go far. So here's a Wren singing.

In woodland
by the Derwent.

I've seen only one.

**Treecreeper
(*Certhia familiaris*)**

(March 2022)

8.

A Closing Miscellany

I could go on and on with one species of bird after another. From being able to recognise hardly any birds less than three years ago I've now accumulated quite a collection of photos, and all from within a few miles of home. I've not become a "twitcher", travelling long distances to get a sight of one specfic bird. No, these birds have come to me. They've simply been there as I've walked in their territories by the river, the pond and the sea.

So to close with, a selection of birds that I've not mentioned earlier or have passed by quickly.

As I said at the beginning, this has done me good. I've lost weight, become more agile and alert; and also have begun to learn, after almost eighty years, how to relax.

My first **Kestrel (*Falco tinnunculus*)**. It was completely unexpected. I was by the shore to the north of the Derwent estuary, the "Old Side". My camera was pointed up into the sky searching for a gull that I'd seen coming in my direction. Suddenly this Kestrel was in the viewfinder; I clicked, and this was the outcome.

Since then I've seen several, The one on the facing page had been sitting in a tree on the fringe of the Crosscannonby reserve when it suddenly flew across to perch in another tree.

A bird that took me by surprise the first time I saw one is the **Little Egret (*Egretta garzetta*)**. I'd never expected to see anything so exotic. Not many years ago it was more or less unheard of in Cumbria, but in recent years has become more common.

My first sighting was in September 2020 near Bowness on Solway, and then a few days later near the same spot I witnessed this dance.

What it was all in aid of I'm not sure. Maybe it was some kind of competitive mating dance. If so, it looked very much as though the female (assuming that the left-hand bird was female) was walking away from both of them. But this was September, not Spring, so I was far from certain and still am.

Since then I've often photographed them at Workington, by the river, the Pond, the estuary and the old harbour. My best photo-session one was in February 2022 on the Mill Field near the Yearl weir. This bird let me take photographs for more than twenty-five minutes. Here are just three of the sequence.

My first view of the bird was as it waded in the mill race, then explored the bank. Food seemed to be on its mind, but there were no catches.

After about five minutes it decided that the wider expanse of water above the weir was a better place, but it didn't find anything to eat there either.

There was a little flying around between the bank and the trees lodged on the weir but eventually the grassy bank of the mill race beckoned again.

After another exploration further down the stream it wandered around the field for a few minutes before deciding to march away and leave me.

And how could I possibly finish without a **Robin** or two (or three)?
(*Erithacus rubecula*)

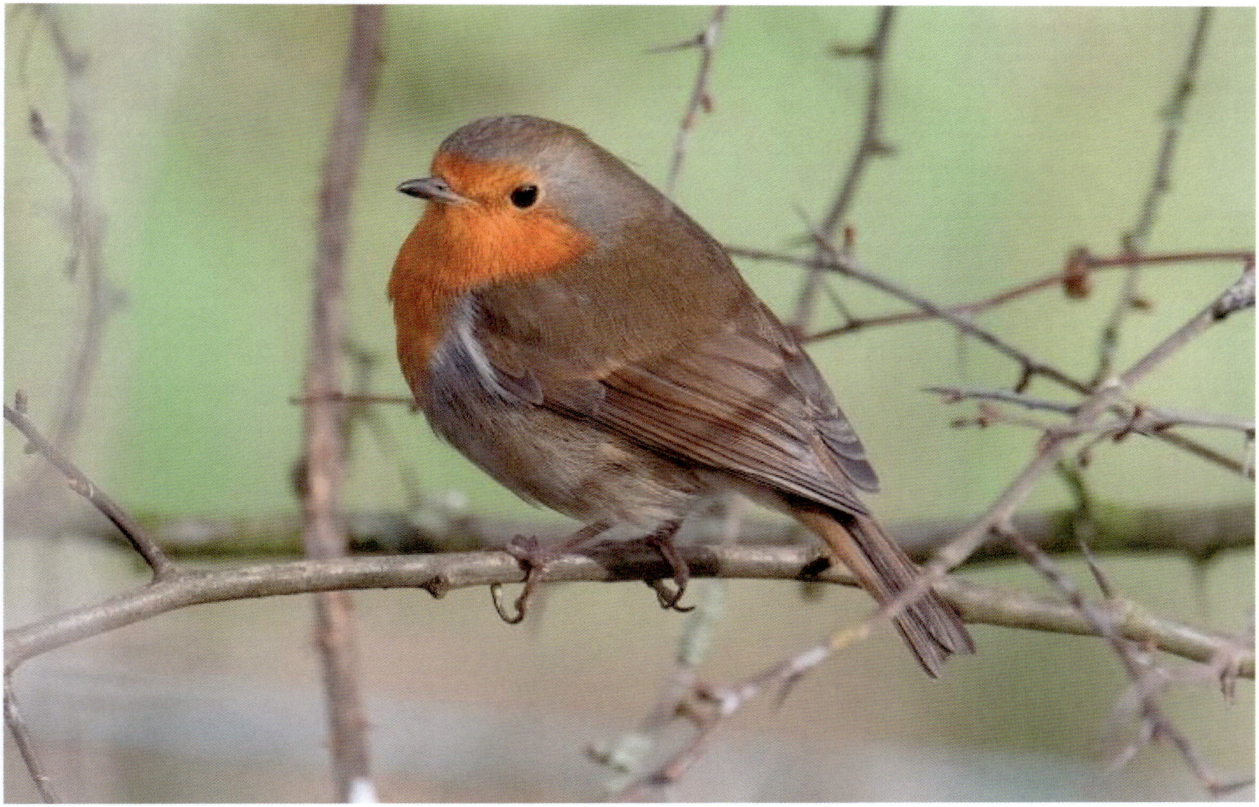

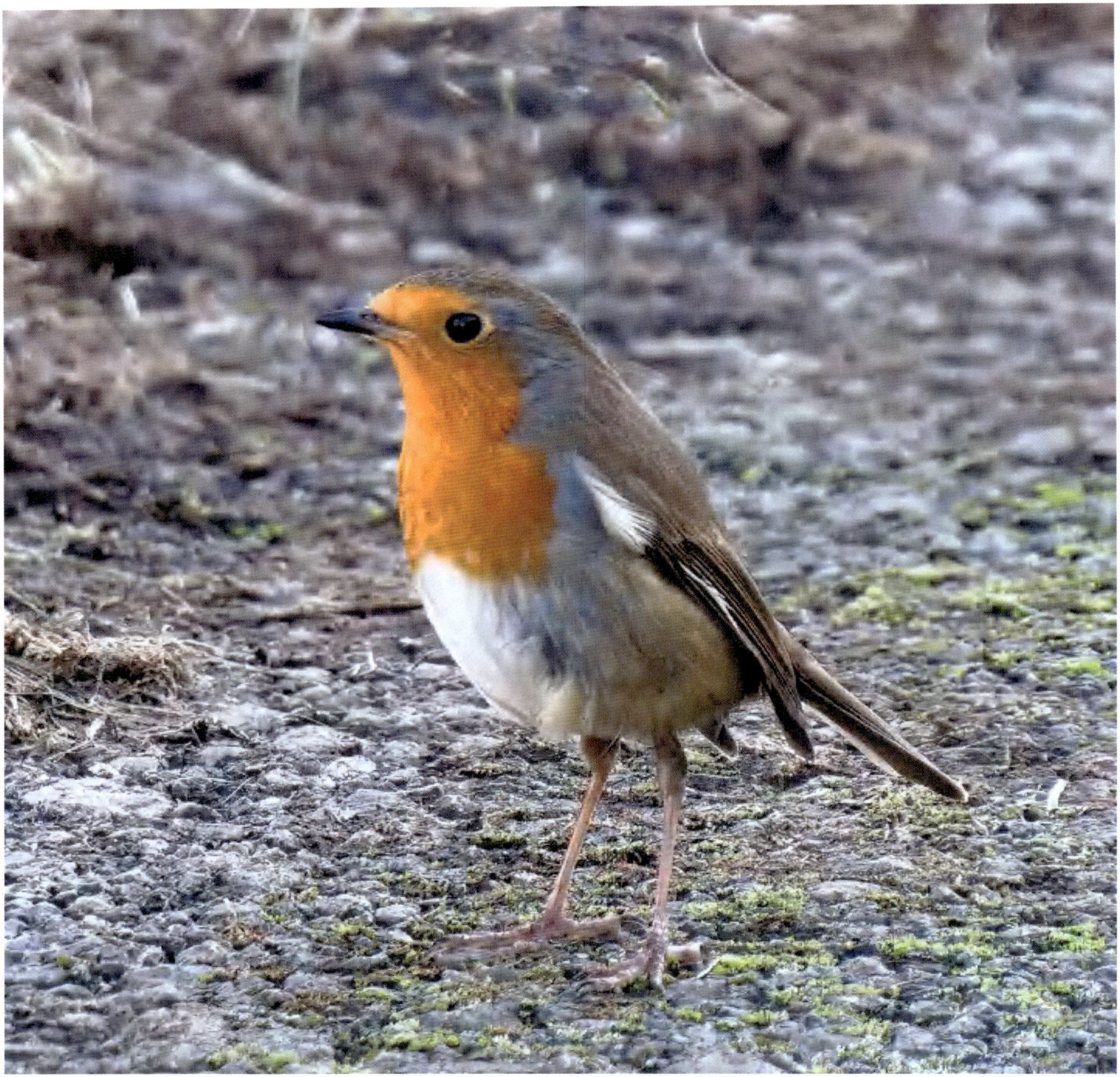

A Few Pages for Notes

Printed in Poland
by Amazon Fulfillment
Poland Sp. z o.o., Wrocław